CUSTOMER

SERVICE

"What About Me?"

Authored by
DonnaMarie

Dedicated to

To all the hardworking individuals who do their best to satisfy the needs of their customers.

INTRODUCTION

No business will ever be successful without *good customer service* and that means *the customer is always right.* How many times have you heard this cliché? If you work in a service related industry, you've heard it more times than you care to remember and providing the best customer service is, or at least should be, second nature to you. There's no argument to the first part; a business will not succeed if its foundation is based on poor service because society has come to expect more. Consumers want what they want, when they want it and in the manner they want it and they don't necessarily care about the person delivering it as long as their needs are met. After more than thirty years in an industry geared toward total customer satisfaction, I finally woke up one day and asked, *"What about me?"*

This booklet is about you, the employee who deals with the public all day long and wants to go home at the end of the day feeling like more than a wet, worthless dishrag. You want to provide the very best assistance to everyone you meet, but *the customer is not always right* and the challenges are often overwhelming and unrewarding. How do you overcome the obstacles?

Let's cover some hurdles a Customer Service Representative faces routinely and take a look at some scenarios from different types of businesses and analyze them. They are all true incidents, but the names are changed to protect the *guilty*.

THE RUDE ONE

Rudeness is simply not acceptable in any form, but unfortunately it runs rampant in our society in all ages and all walks of life. Arrogance has no boundaries and it's one, if not the toughest, obstacle to overcome because every action has a reaction and our human nature directs us to be rude back when someone is bad-mannered to us. It's a self-conscious defense mechanism because throughout the evolution of mankind, it is the strongest who survive and striking out at the weak comes naturally to all us.

Scenario One

Mrs. Peterson walks into Nature's Best Grocery Store pushing her carriage past other shoppers, oblivious to the fact that she bumps them as she goes by. She's on a mission to complete her grocery list in record time and return home to watch her soap operas. Walter is on Aisle Three, making a futile attempt to clean up a broken jar of molasses. He has followed company procedure and put up the aisle cones to block passage until the broken glass is removed and the floor is no longer sticky. His brand new slacks will now have a super bee following when he walks outside, so he's not in the best mood, but he is doing his job and keeping it to himself. Mrs. Peterson either does not see the barriers or she has totally ignored them because she is coming right toward him and only stops when her carriage nudges his foot.

"Excuse me," she says to him as she approaches. "Hand me that bottle of maple syrup on the top shelf. I can't reach it."

Walter doesn't want to be rude, so he smiles and hands her the syrup which she literally grabs from his hand and begins to read the label. Then she says

7

to him, "I don't want this, give me that other one up there." In the meantime, she puts the one she has in her hand on the first shelf with another product. Walter does as he is told, but this time without the smile, and passes her the second bottle which she takes without a 'thank you'.

In the meantime, he notices that other customers see her in the aisle and are beginning to pass the barrier, so he says, "Excuse me, but this aisle is closed. I'll have it cleaned and it will be open in just a few minutes." They listen to him, but Mrs. Peterson does not.

"I'm not done here," she says to him, and then adds, "How can you charge so much for this? Look at the price on it, will you? The bottle is smaller and it's gone up twenty cents. Do you think I'm stupid?"

Walters tries to say something, but she has no intention of listening and just keeps rambling on about *the price. There's nothing he wants more at the moment than to shout back at her and tell her to, "Shut up!" He is tempted to push the cart back into her, but he maintains control.*

Well, it's obvious that Walter got himself into a situation with this one and he's wondering how to get out it and away from her.

First of all, let's congratulate Walter for maintaining his cool. Technically, he didn't do anything wrong. He was just doing his job cleaning the aisle, so it was safe for customers to reenter.

The scene could be avoided altogether, however, if he was pro-active when he saw Mrs. Peterson go around the cones. Of course, it's an inconvenience, but the minute she entered the aisle, it was unsafe for her to be there. In hindsight, it would be better for him to put down the mop and walk toward her with the largest grin he could muster and ask her what he could do to help her. When she persists on passing, he should tell her about the floor and when that failed, he should *be creative*! He could tell her that the spilled product would ruin her shoes, or the odor might make her ill, but she can continue to shop and come back to that aisle in a few minutes. If that didn't work, he could tell her he would be more than happy to get her what she needs while she waits right there. She might continue to be rude, but he is now firm without being aggressive, or offensive, and he will feel better about himself if he is in control of the situation and still providing her with the service she expects and deserves.

Most importantly, he should not give in and allow her to walk into an unsafe environment. He should keep smiling, without a smirk, or rolling eyes. Offensive body language is not acceptable.

When you're faced with this type of customer, maintain the higher standard by making it your personal challenge to remain calm and consistent in your service. We all like winning and as you look at someone like this, listen to the rudeness, remind yourself that, like Walter, you will win if you maintain control! Sometimes success shows itself in minute ways, perhaps for Walter, it was keeping her from asking for his manager, or preventing her from getting hurt in his aisle which would certainly have consequences for him. If you're really lucky, she'll leave also feeling a winner, but don't hold your breath on that one.

THE GLUTTON

We all know this customer, the one who wants everything for nothing. If they don't get it for nothing, they fail and as mentioned in the previous section, everyone wants to be a winner. Before you harshly judge this type of person, take a good look deep inside yourself and be honest. Aren't we all the same? How many times have you entered a drawing knowing you had no use for the prize? We all do it and when we win, we are excited to receive the prize even if we don't need it, or want it. The following scenario is one that many of us can relate to.

Scenario Two

Linda works on commission for XYZ Insurance Company and was asked by her supervisor to attend a Business Exposition. Sales are down and the company is on a mission to cut back on expenses, so she is told she will work the shift alone in an effort to keep the salaried employees on the phones and in the office. She will be required to sit at a table and give out literature and answer questions. Rather than seeing this as a networking opportunity, she looks at it as wasted time when she could be increasing her monthly commissions; therefore, she is already in a poor mood when she arrives.

The table was previously set up for her and she notices the abundance of promotional items on the table for attendees to take. There's also an extravagant raffle item that she knows cost the company a great deal of money. She is immediately offended that she was reminded by her supervisor of the company's cutbacks because this appears to her as a waste of time and money.

It doesn't take long for a rush of people to approach her table and they are picking up the free items and putting their names into the box for the drawing. She notices that several people are entering their names more than once and many of them take more than one of the table items. One woman blatantly takes a handful of pens and puts them in her purse and Linda feels this is inappropriate, so she tells the woman that only one item is allowed per person. The woman is offended, puts the pens back on the table and walks away in silence.

It's obvious that Linda isn't having a good day because she is totally absorbed in her own feelings and asking, "What about me?" She is clearly not seeing the full picture and there is no doubt, she will go home after her shift feeling terrible about everything in general.

First of all, Linda's attitude is setting her up for failure. She should be smiling sincerely and talking to each person that comes to her table, encouraging them to converse with her. Rather than seeing them as greedy people trying to take the freebies, she should see them as potential clients, or referral sources. Without a doubt, her body language will give her away and people will take their items and leave her presence as quickly as possible.

What about the lady taking the pens? What if Linda gave her a huge smile and said, "Oh, I'm so glad you're taking the pens. I hope you're going to give them out for me. Do you need some more?" She might even add, "Would you mind handing out my business cards with those? I would really appreciate it." At that point, the woman could, and probably would, easily come back with a response, telling her why she needed the pens, maybe she's a teacher, or a waitress and they always need pens. It doesn't matter because it's free advertising and Linda had the opportunity to take advantage of a situation, but instead saw it in a negative light. Promotional items are a great way to get a company's name out to the public and the pens will surely pass from one hand to another many times over.

Without realizing it, Linda became THE GLUTTON when she selfishly tried to hang on to the items. She also became THE RUDE ONE when she chastised the woman for taking the pens.

Too often we forget to look at the full picture, seeing instead only the situation at hand. It wasn't up to Linda to decide what to give away for the company, nor was it up to Linda to even attend the Business Exposition. She was chosen for a reason that completely slipped by her. The company gave her the opportunity to make new contacts, grow her referral base, and get her own name out there. Her supervisor placed her in a garden of flowers, ready to be picked and she saw only the weeds.

Attitude is like the weather, make yours a sunny one and you will soon realize that, "What about me?" can turn into a great day when you are in control. *Go for it!*

THE BLANK STARE

This customer is a challenge! No matter how hard you try, you just can't get through to him or her. You give a set of instructions that are important and you know they're not understood, so you repeat them again, and even again, still nothing. Maybe you'll get a question, or two, but no matter how many times you try, it just doesn't penetrate. You know the customer will be back and furious if something doesn't work properly, or the end result is different than expected. What do you do? How do you get through to that customer without wanting to pull out your own hair? It isn't easy, but it's also not impossible.

Scenario Three

It's Open House at John Smith Elementary School and Mary, an Administrative Assistant, is assigned to sit at the Welcome Desk and greet the parents as they come in with their children to visit the

school. She looks forward to a day away from her

normal duties, so she's cheerful and having fun with

everyone who comes in, that is, until she meets Mrs.

Suarez, who approaches her desk with her three

young children.

"Good Morning! Welcome to John Smith

Elementary," Mary says to her cheerfully. Mrs.

Suarez awkwardly stands there smiling, but she does

not respond, so Mary continues to speak. "This is a

map of our school and this little 'X' on it is where you

are right now. Just follow the arrows on the map until

you visit each classroom for five minutes. When you

are finished, go to the Cafeteria, then the

Gymnasium, and finally the Auditorium where the

teachers are divided by grades. The class's rosters

are posted on the north wall, so find your child's name

and proceed to the assigned teacher and check in. Please enjoy yourself...Next!"

Mrs. Suarez just stands there with a blank stare on her face and Mary has no idea why. Rather than ask her, she cranes her neck around the mother to ask for the next family in line. Mrs. Suarez doesn't move and she leans over toward Mary and with a heavy accent asks, "What do I do now?"

Mary patiently repeats the exact instructions and when she finishes, Mrs. Suarez asks, "Which way do I go?" By now, Mary is getting agitated. How much more specific could she be? She goes over it again, but this time there's no cheeriness and without realizing it, Mary's voice is now escalated and she is speaking to Mrs. Suarez as if she was deaf.

Mrs. Suarez finally nods her head that she understands, takes the map and heads down the hallway in the opposite direction. Mary, now exasperated, jumps up from her seat and yells out to

her to stop!

Okay, where did Mary go wrong, or did she? She started off doing everything correctly. She was cheerful, organized, had great intentions and gave specific instructions. It was only when Mrs. Suarez didn't understand them that the situation went south. When Mrs. Suarez gave Mary the first *deer in the headlights* look, why didn't Mary ask her if she understood? By repeating the instructions exactly as she did the first time, Mary only added to the confusion, paraphrasing them the second time would be better.

Also, it never occurred to Mary that Mrs. Suarez didn't speak English fluently and maybe the instructions contained words that were not yet in the mother's vocabulary. Rather than repeat the directives in simpler language, Mary spoke louder which is a natural tendency for many of us to do, but Mrs. Suarez wasn't deaf; she simply didn't understand what she was being told.

As an Administrative Assistant, this was probably not the first time Mary ran into a situation where a parent didn't have a mastery of the English language. In this case, Mrs. Suarez's native language was Spanish, and we presume that Mary spoke only English. There may be someone close by that speaks Spanish and could translate, but Mary never tried to get anyone because it simply didn't occur to her to do so.

At the very least, Mary should excuse herself for a minute and walk Mrs. Suarez to the first classroom which was only a few feet down the hall. At that point, she could explain to the teacher that Mrs. Suarez was having difficulty and perhaps someone could help her to the next station and so on. It's doubtful that returning to her desk, Mary would face any unhappy parents waiting their turn because they watched her go the extra mile and she would still be in her cheerful mood for the remaining families. Unfortunately, it didn't go that way and Mrs. Suarez was embarrassed and confused while Mary was now frustrated and in a poor mood.

We can't read someone else's mind and we should never presume that they comprehend what we are trying to communicate. One simple question, *"Do you understand?"* speaks volumes and opens the door to better communication and less stress for everyone involved.

THE KNOW IT ALL

This is by far one of the most annoying of all customer types. It doesn't matter what we say, this person will know more than we do, or at least want us to think that way. This personality type finds it difficult to give anyone else credit for knowing anything. If you say it's black, this individual will insist that it's white and so forth.

Scenario Four

Edwin is a waiter at Italian Delight Restaurant and although he has worked there for four years, he works part-time, so he can attend the local college, therefore, he doesn't have the opportunity to meet some of the regulars who eat there. Tonight, however, his class was cancelled, so he was able to cover another employee's shift.

Mr. & Mrs. Smith come into the restaurant and the hostess seats them at their favorite table. Edwin approaches the table and introduces himself and gives them the list of specials for the evening. Mr. Smith interrupts him and tells him he must have the wrong list because lasagna is always a special on Tuesday nights and he didn't mention it. Edwin politely tells him that it is not available this evening, but Mr. Smith again states that he must have incorrect information because that's the way it has been for the past two years.

Mrs. Smith intervenes and says she would like something different tonight anyway. She wants the chicken parmesan and a salad with the house dressing. Mr. Smith agrees to the same, but says he wants his dressing made with less vinegar. Edwin politely explains that the base of the dressing is made with olive oil and lemon juice and there is no vinegar.

Also, it is premade and cannot be changed.

Immediately, Mr. Smith is on the defensive and insists

he has ordered it this way for two years and that's

how he wants it tonight. Again, Edwin tells him he

could not order it that way because that's not how it

was made and he also tells Mr. Smith that he has

worked for this restaurant for four years and knows

exactly how they make it. Mr. Smith will not let it go,

insinuates that Edwin is not telling the truth about his

length of employment and asks to see the manager.

Mrs. Smith is now feeling uncomfortable and the

guests at the surrounding tables are listening to the

disagreement. Edwin's evening has drastically

bombed over a couple of tablespoons of salad

dressing!

What was Edwin thinking? He was correct

about the ingredients in the dressing, but it doesn't

matter because Mr. Smith strongly believed otherwise and maybe he did order it that way in the past. It does not matter if he did, *or did not*, because he believed he did and he believed he got what he asked for and he was not going to change his mind for Edwin.

All Edwin had to do to avoid the entire conflict was say, "I'll check with the kitchen, I'm sure they will know what you're asking for and I'll be happy to bring it to you." Chances are the kitchen had this request from him before, or they could put something together quickly to satisfy him. Unfortunately, Edwin is now going to hear from his supervisor about the incident and the restaurant may lose the Smiths as regular customers. Also, let's not forget the surrounding customers who also didn't know Edwin. Who do you think they will believe? I would hate to believe that I lost my job over a little lemon juice!

You can't win with people like this, so you need to appease them and let them feel as if you are truly making an attempt to meet their needs. In some instances, you should even compliment their knowledge if the situation warrants it. Don't let your pride get in the way because the consequences aren't worth the risk. Consider what's at stake before you decide to take a stand because being right doesn't always mean you win the battle.

"What about me?" you ask. You will have peace of mind when you go home at the end of your day knowing that you are in the winner's circle, not in your supervisor's office trying to explain the saga of two tablespoons of salad dressing!

SHORT-FUSED AND IRATE

Anger is handled differently by each of us and it's not to be taken lightly. Entire educational courses are devoted to Anger Management and many of them assigned by the courts after an incident occurs and it is too late. *Do not* underestimate the potential seriousness of someone angered or under severe stress. Learn to read the signs and defuse the situation before it escalates out of control.

Scenario Five

Al is a relatively new employee at Tire Mart which is a reputable company in town and the owner has been in business for several years. Although he is new at his job, he completed his training in record time, impressing his boss and co-workers with his thorough and detailed work ethics.

Today he is changing the tire on a Jeep when a vehicle speeds into the parking lot, skids to a stop in front of the garage and a middle-aged man jumps out and quickly approaches the open garage door. Al recognizes the truck as one he worked on the day before and remembers the man as the owner. Only employees are allowed to enter the garage, but Mr. Jones storms in anyway, his face is bright red and his fists are clenched. He walks up to Al and before any spoken words, Al knows there is something drastically wrong because this man is extremely irate.

Mr. Jones begins shouting at Al, telling him that he almost had the worst accident of his life, which nearly killed his entire family. Al tries to ask him what happened, but Mr. Jones keeps ranting on, threatening to sue the Tire Mart and Al personally because his tires weren't balanced properly and it was all Al's fault. He takes a threatening step toward

*Al and continues his tirade. Al is a large young man
and not easily intimidated, so he stands taller and
glares back at Mr. Jones, then defensively asks,
"What's your problem?"*

*The other employees stop working and all eyes
are on the two men, curious to see what will happen
next. The supervisor steps up to them and in a low,
non-threatening voice asks Mr. Jones to step into the
office to tell him what happened. He tells Al to get
back to work, but Al objects and starts to follow them
anyway. His supervisor turns and tells him once
again to stay there and get back to work.*

Fortunately for Al, his supervisor intervened
before the encounter went completely out of control.
Anger overrules sensibility and when faced with a life-
threatening situation for his family, Mr. Jones reacted
to the scare with emotion, blaming the technician for

the error. Al, on the other hand, reacted defensively to the situation, putting out aggressive signals to Mr. Jones, which only made him angrier. If Al followed his supervisor and Mr. Jones into the office, the situation would not be resolved because it was Al that Mr. Jones blamed. The supervisor had a much better chance of defusing the conflict and maybe later on, *or maybe not*, he would bring Al into it.

First and foremost, when put into a situation with an irate person, remain calm! Listen, show empathy, and let your body language portray the same. Don't shout back, instead speak more softly, and slow down your words, so they can be absorbed. Avoid threatening gestures, such as moving closer to the person, or speaking animatedly with your hands.

Don't demand, instead ask the person to follow you into an office or other private area, so you can listen and try to resolve the problem. By all means, offer to get your manager, or supervisor. Again, remember to remain calm and don't take it personally!

Some people are short-fused by character, others lose control when faced with situations they cannot manage, but whatever the cause, it is up to you as an employee to handle it professionally. Always, and I repeat, *always*, tell your supervisor of the incident in the event the customer decides to take it further, or another employee inadvertently slips the information before you reveal it. Do not ever let your boss be blind-sided because the "What about me?" will leave you on the down side.

I WANT IT YESTERDAY

I love these people because this type of person throws me into a 'get it done' pace that will follow me the remainder of the day. Sometimes, there's a legitimate need to get something in a hurry, but many times it's a *want* rather than a *need.* As far as you are concerned, just get it for the customer as soon as you can because it's not your place to decide if the customer is exaggerating, or overreacting. If you fight it, you'll add more stress to yourself and that's what we're trying to eliminate here.

Scenario Six

Lucy is a Customer Service Representative at Best National Bank and she is watching the clock today because she is taking her son to his first little league game right after work. The bank lobby closes at four o'clock, but she is scheduled to work until four-

thirty. She'll be cutting it close, but she can still make

it if nothing delays her. At three-thirty, Mrs. Nelson

enters the bank and, as always, refuses to see

anyone except her favorite Customer Service

Representative. Lucy knows from experience that a

visit from Mrs. Nelson always comes with a crisis,

usually a self-induced one and from the woman's

demeanor; Lucy assumes that today is no different.

She smiles sincerely to the customer, but her

stomach is already in a knot.

     Mrs. Nelson tells Lucy that there is a problem

with her Social Security and she received a letter

asking for two years of prior bank statements.

Although Lucy has the authority and the capability to

print the statements, it is the bank's normal procedure

to have these actions done by a centralized

Operations Center. Lucy knows from experience that

it will be at least a three day turnaround time, so she

tells this to Mrs. Nelson and silently breathes a sigh of relief that she is off the hook.

Mrs. Nelson becomes clearly upset and lets Lucy know that this is unacceptable. She is a longtime bank customer and knows that the statements can be printed from the branch and she wants to wait for them. Lucy explains the bank's procedure and they argue for nearly twenty minutes until the manager comes over to ask if there is a problem. Mrs. Nelson tells him that she needs the statements today and she is willing to sit there for as long as it takes to get them. The manager looks at Lucy and tells her to print them up for Mrs. Nelson. It is now four o'clock and the lobby doors are locked, but Lucy does as she is told. While they are printing, Mrs. Nelson shows Lucy the letter she received and asks her to fax the statements to the number provided. Lucy reads the letter and sees that the

Social Security Administration actually gave her 30

days to produce the statements, but, they are already

printing. Lucy agreed to get them done, so now she

is locked into the task. She is late for her son's game.

Lucy had good intentions; she wanted to satisfy Mrs. Nelson and she did as her manager asked without question, but she became the loser because she failed to identify the real needs of her customer. Mrs. Nelson told her right away about the letter, so why didn't she ask to see it? Instead, she wasted twenty minutes arguing with the woman over bank procedure when Mrs. Nelson didn't care how it happened, she just wanted it done and wanted it done right away.

A simpler way to handle this situation would be to read the letter firsthand if it is available and determine the best way to handle it. Point out the specifics of the letter to the customer, including the requested timeframe. Show empathy and assure your customer that you will take responsibility to make sure this is done. This may require that you do it yourself, or that you personally follow-up regarding the completion of the task. Either way, you own the situation and it's important for your customer to know that. In this case, Mrs. Nelson doesn't want to hear that someone she doesn't know is going to handle this from miles away. It's Lucy she has faith in, so Lucy needs to step up to the plate and handle it.

Valuable time was lost because Lucy didn't immediately begin printing some of the statements, showing Mrs. Nelson that it was under control. If she showed the customer she was doing it right away, Lucy could then explain that the bank was closing, however, the task would still be in the works and she would call Mrs. Nelson in the morning to give her an update. Perhaps the Operations Center was in another time zone; therefore, their staff would be working long after Lucy's branch closed. Better yet, Mrs. Nelson might be thrilled to know it was open twenty-four hours and someone there would do it during the night. A call to the Operations Center in front of Mrs. Nelson would go a long way in building her confidence that it was under control. Better yet, of course, would be if Lucy did it herself. There was a fax number on the letter, so Lucy could add that she would be glad to fax them out for her and offer Mrs. Nelson a copy of the fax receipt for her records.

Her son's first little league game was Lucy's top priority, but Mrs. Nelson's main concern was the fear of losing her social security. These are equally important.

Remember to identify the problem, own the problem and follow it through and do not be afraid to ask another employee, another department, or even your manager for help if you cannot get the job done in the timely manner your customer is requesting.

The customer does not always know what is needed which is why they are coming to you in the first place. Show that you understand the situation and give them the confidence that you will get it done. The customer will leave satisfied and you will feel great knowing you completed the task at hand in the best way possible.

WANT OR NEED?

Basic primal human craving tells us we *want* a cookie, but common sense tells us we don't *need* it. Life will not end without the cookie, nor will life end for the customer who doesn't get everything he *wants*, rather than *needs*. Unfortunately, your job in customer service will quickly end if you don't meet your customer's needs.

Scenario Seven

Josh works for Good-Car Automotive Mall which is one of the largest car dealers in his county. For five consecutive months, he was the Number One salesperson and the dealership awards a substantial bonus to anyone who can maintain that standing for six months in a row. It's the last day of the month and he is tied with another salesperson for First Place. The General Manager just announced at the morning sales meeting that there is one particular vehicle, a convertible on the lot, that has to be moved and anyone who sells it will get double their commission for it. The car is last year's model, overpriced, and has poor consumer ratings. Josh prides himself on his repeat customers and their referrals because he has a reputation for being honest, professional and fits the customer to a vehicle they can both love and afford. This car, a yellow convertible sports car, would not be a choice for his customers.

Josh promised his family a long overdue vacation with his earnings this month, but now he's getting nervous. He called his entire book of business, offering them a deal, but now his list of names is exhausted. The weather is bad and there are no customers on the lot, but then Tom Stetson walks in.

Tom is a middle-aged man who buys a new family vehicle from Josh every three years. There's something a little different about Tom's clothes and mannerism this time and it's only been eighteen months since the last purchase. It doesn't take long for him to tell Josh that he is recently divorced and wants to spruce up his life a little. He wants to trade in his four-door sedan for a two-door coupe that is a little sportier. He spotted a nice black one on the lot and would like to see it. Josh sees his opportunity.

Josh takes him to see the black one and points out the flaws to Tom and because Tom trusts him thoroughly, he is discouraged about the car. He reminds Josh that he doesn't want the same image anymore and, Josh tells him that he has just the vehicle for him. Of course, the minute Tom sees the yellow convertible and Josh shows him all the amenities, he falls in love with it. He hesitates, but it's short-lived after Josh convinces him how it will

change his entire image. Josh knows this is more

than a vehicle, it's a life style change for Tom and it's

not the right car for him, but he is overcome with the

need to win the contest and the bonus. Tom wants

this car; he doesn't need it.

The bonus is won by Josh, the General

Manager is happy because the car is sold and Tom is

ecstatic driving off the lot. It's a win-win for

everybody, or is it? A few weeks later, the car is in

the shop, the General Manager is being harassed

with complaint calls about the vehicle and Josh is no

longer taking Tom's calls because he is being blamed

for selling him a lemon. The customer really wanted

and needed the two-door black sedan.

Tom will probably return less than a year later

to trade in the convertible after he realizes that it is

the wrong vehicle for him, but more than likely, he will either not return to that dealership, or he will not seek out Josh. In years past, he referred a minimum of two friends per year to Josh, who in turn each referred two more. The dominoes are down; the referrals from this source are over.

In any service industry, it is important to identify the customer's needs. Separate those needs from their wants and give honest pros and cons. Be upfront and tell the truth, earn their trust and respect. Successful companies are built on solid foundations of customer loyalty; be part of building the castle, not bringing it down. When you go home at night and look in the mirror, you'll ask, "What about me?" The answer will be, "I'm happy."

THE INTIMIDATOR

Intimidation comes in many forms. It may be verbal, physical, or both. A person is verbally intimidating when they pressure you with attitude, or threats. "If you don't do this, I will do that..." or it can be a person who consistently *name drops*.

Physical intimidation, however, may be a simple step forward entering the immediate space around you. Your personal space generally extends to one arm's length from your body, but in some cases the difference can be greater. When someone leans over your desk toward you, this is an intimidating movement.

This is adult bullying and it's not pleasant to be on the receiving end of it. What do you do about it?

Scenario Eight

Miranda is an Executive Assistant at Anywhere Corporation. She is the official GATEKEEPER who controls and screens every telephone call and visitor for Mr. Sanders, the CEO. She is professional, trustworthy and loyal to the corporation.

Mr. Sanders is hosting an enormous fundraiser that will be attended by local politicians, celebrities, and community leaders. The guest list is a 'who's who' and limited to invitation only.

Early Monday morning, Miranda takes a call from Mr. Marshall and before he can say anything, she tells him that Mr. Sanders is in a meeting, but she will be glad to give him a message when he contacts her. Mr. Marshall tells her that she is the one he wants to speak to because his invitation had not yet arrived.

Jim Marshall is the owner of a local radio

station and Miranda is aware that he was previously

invited to many functions hosted by Mr. Sanders, but

he is not on the list for this one because it is so

limited. She is also familiar with his brash, overt

personality and is cautious with her answer, so she

tells him that the affair is extremely small and limited

to a specialized circle of individuals with strong ties to

the charity.

He interrupts her and tells her that there must

be a mistake because he does have ties to the charity

and has cancelled checks to prove it. He also tells

her that the mayor has personally asked him if he was

attending because he wanted to meet with him.

Miranda responds that she will speak to Mr. Sanders

and get back with him, but Mr. Marshall tells her not to

bother him with the matter because he will just get a

ticket through Commissioner Danz. Miranda explains

that there are no available tickets and Mr. Sanders

has full control. The conversation goes on for several

minutes and Mr. Marshall drops one name after

another. When Miranda still doesn't offer him a

means to obtain a ticket, he tells her that he doesn't

like her attitude and plans to discuss it with Mr.

Sanders. He hangs up on her and she now worried

about her job.

Later that afternoon, she receives a bouquet of

flowers from Mr. Marshall with a thank you note

regarding the ticket he knows she will obtain for him.

She decides not to call him until she speaks to Mr.

Sanders who tells her not to worry about it.

The next morning, however, Mr. Marshall

comes to the office and blatantly flirts with her and

reminds her of the flowers. He leans over her desk

and tells her that he knows people who can help her

advance in her career after Mr. Sanders retires which

he knows to be sooner than she thinks. She ignores
his advances and tells him that she will tell Mr.
Sanders to call him. This angers him and as he
leaves, he tells her that he will have her job for this.
She is upset, but remains professional and in control.

Congratulations to Miranda because she did everything right! She maintained her composure at all times, didn't make promises she couldn't keep, informed her boss of the situation and wasn't at all impressed with the flowers or name dropping. She was truly professional and in control throughout the ordeal.

This is not an easy personality to face, but the key word is *self-control*. Don't give in to demands that you shouldn't, or can't do. Have patience, tolerate the situation, and don't take it personally. You're not a doormat, nor should you be treated as one, but if you give in to the pressures, or show your weakness, one

situation will turn into another and then another.

JUST PLAIN NASTY

Hopefully, this customer will be few and far between for you. I'm speaking about the person who is physically dirty, sick, or just plain nasty! You're in a service related industry and you are required to wait on him.

Scenario Nine

Ted is one of four assistant librarians in the Nowhere County Public Library. It's a large library and very busy on most days, especially toward the weekend. Every Friday afternoon, Sam comes into the library and sits at one of the tables reading for an hour or so. Ted and the other assistants avoid him at all cost because he is physically offensive. His white hair and beard are untrimmed, his clothes are stained and torn, his worn shoes are dirty and he smells foul. He coughs continually without putting his hand over his mouth and has open sores on his arms. Sam is nasty!

This particular Friday, Sam is looking for a particular magazine and is having trouble locating it. He approaches the work area where the assistants are stationed and Ted notices that he is suddenly alone because his three co-workers have conveniently disappeared. Sam approaches Ted and tells him he can't locate the magazine and asks him for help. Not realizing what he was doing, Ted unconsciously took a step backward to avoid the bad breath. Sam coughs, leaving moisture spots on the counter. Ted rudely points to the magazine rack and tells him that if it's not there, then they don't have it. He turns his back to Sam and ignores him.

First of all, shame on the three assistants who left Ted stranded! We can't pick and choose who we help and who we don't. They didn't just abandon Ted, they abandoned their duty and that is never acceptable.

As for Ted, it is only natural that we back away from foul odors, but to be obvious about it is rude. Keep a jar of hard mint candies, or a package of gum to offer. When Sam coughed, a simple gesture of handing him a tissue might prevent the unsanitary spray on the counter.

You are never expected to place yourself in an unhealthy situation. In Sam's case, the illness can be seen and it causes fear, but how many times are we exposed to illnesses that we can't see. Keep anti-bacterial wipes close at hand to wipe down your work area several times during the day and use hand sanitizer often.

Most importantly, don't judge someone like Sam harshly without knowing the full story. There's more to the above scenario: *Sam is a retired college professor who lost his wife tragically and they had no children. He has no family and was recently diagnosed with Stage Four cancer. He knows his time is limited and it will not be long before he is bathed daily, dressed in clean clothes and confined to a hospital; until then he just does not care.* If you want to help, do it in small ways, with a smile, a tissue, a mint, even a fresh shirt that you just happen to have for him, but do not avoid him, do not abandon your service responsibilities and *sanitize, sanitize, sanitize.*

JUST SAY NO!

What if you're asked to do something against your company's policy or worse yet, something illegal? How do you handle it? What do you say? Who do you tell? It's easy for a parent to tell a child to "say no", but what about us as adults? It's more complicated, or is it?

Scenario Ten

Maggie is a new teller at Mytown Community Bank and she is getting to know her customers. Pete Stanton walks to her window and introduces himself and hands her his driver's license. He wants to deposit a check into his personal account and he gives her the check and deposit slip. Maggie looks at the check and it is made out to his business account, not to him personally, so she tells him that he needs to deposit the check into the business account. He tells her he doesn't want to do that and the teller

before her never had a problem with it. Maggie is

patient and takes the time to explain that he could

deposit the check into the business account and then

write a check to himself from that account, or

withdraw it in cash. He is adamant that he doesn't

want to put it into the business account and states

that it's none of the IRS's business where his money

originates. Maggie offers to get her supervisor, but he

concedes and she deposits the check into the

business account. Throughout the ordeal, Pete

remained pleasant, so Maggie feels comfortable with

the outcome and thinks it's over.

Before Pete leaves, however, he asks her how

much money he can deposit before it's reported to the

IRS? She asks him why he is questioning this, but he

evades answering her and hands over a brown bag

with cash and another deposit slip to a third account.

Maggie verifies that he is the owner of the account, but she notices that he routinely deposits $7,500 approximately every three or four days. She pulls up the transactions and notices they are all cash deposits. Maggie is now very uncomfortable with this customer, so she excuses herself under pretense of getting another pen and goes to the Teller Supervisor who joins her at the teller window and asks Pete pointedly where he obtained the cash, telling him it is a routine question when no paper trail is involved. Pete again asks how much cash he can deposit before the IRS would take notice. Both the Teller Supervisor and Maggie avoid answering the question directly, but the Supervisor states with a smile that the IRS can monitor all transactions. He tells her it's no one's business and refuses to disclose where the money came from and he will not fill out any questionnaire, he says. Pete tells her to make sure *the bank doesn't report him to the IRS. He takes the*

money back and leaves.

There are red flags all over this. Maggie did the right thing when she refused to deposit the business check into his personal account. Maybe the teller before her did do it, but that does not make it right and, who knows, maybe the teller is no longer there because she failed to follow bank procedures!

When Pete asked her the question about cash deposits, he was asking her to tell him how to structure money. This is unlawful and Maggie was right when she brought her supervisor into it. Neither of them gave into his demands. They said 'NO' without actually saying the word itself. Procedures were followed and now it is up to Maggie and the Teller Supervisor to notify their next level upward and the appropriate bank personnel or department who will initiate an investigation.

Saying 'NO' is not always easy, but the consequences for doing the alternative will be much more difficult to handle. If it's illegal, or against your company's policy, DON'T DO IT and report it to your supervisor immediately.

SUMMARY

As mentioned in the introduction, this is about *you*, the Customer Service Employee who works with the public, wants to be good at what you do, but has the desire and the right to go home after your shift feeling good about yourself.

It's okay to ask, "What about me?" You work hard and take pride in what you do, so do it the *right* way and do it the *smart* way.

Customer Service is basic common sense. Treat the person in front of you the same way you want to be treated. Welcome your customer as if you were inviting a friend into your home and treat that customer as you would treat your friend. Identify their needs and meet their demands if possible, but understand that you will not always be able to give what's asked of you. Do not take it personal; instead accept the challenge to overcome the obstacles presented to you.

If you take nothing out of this short lesson except one thing, remember that you are the foundation of a successful business. Good employers and most of them truly are, will appreciate your hard work, support you and understand that from time to time, you may ask, *"What about me?"* The answer is you will feel good about yourself when you get up in the morning and good about yourself when you go home at night because you know you did the very best you could do.

Do not take the hurdles as personal assaults; instead accept them as a challenge and a means to becoming a stronger person and a better employee. *Enjoy your job* and do 'not' be afraid to ask yourself, *"What about me?"* You will like the answer...

Acknowledgement

A special acknowledgement goes to every employer who understands that anyone can provide customer service, but GREAT customer service comes with challenges and a special dedication from the employees who provide it. They are the foundation for your success and you deserve a special 'thank you' for your support and understanding when asked,

"What about me?"

Made in the USA
Columbia, SC
17 October 2022

69564581R00037